BLUE

Other Books in the Series:

Colours by Giovanna Ranaldi

Red by Valentina Zucchi and Paolo D'Altan

White by Valentina Zucchi and Francesca Zoboli

Black by Valentina Zucchi and Francesca Zoboli

Yellow by Valentina Zucchi and Sylvie Bello

Green by Valentina Zucchi and Angela Leon

BLUE

BY VALENTINA ZUCCHI
AND VIOLA NICCOLAI

Translated from the Italian
by Katherine Gregor

René Magritte, *The Infinite Recognition* (1963), Private Collection

CONTENTS

LOOKING AT BLUE

'You must look at all of life with the eyes of a child.' (Henri Matisse, 1953)

The rainbow is an extraordinary phenomenon: a natural collection of colour samples that occurs in specific light and weather conditions. Nobody has ever managed to get close to it and touch it, but if we ever stretch our imaginations and make such a thing happen, perhaps we would have the chance to pick up the colours, one by one, and examine them carefully, discover them and enjoy them.

Humans have always been fascinated by colours and have tried to create and use them since the dawn of time. This is why every colour has a story to tell, and in this series of books, we have tried to share some of those stories with you. The books originated at the Palazzo Vecchio, in Florence, where the Associazione MUS.E works constantly to restore works of art to their authentic colours, with the support of Giotto-FILA, who actually manufacture colours. Thank you, Giotto-FILA.

This book examines blue, perhaps the best-loved colour of all. Blue – like velvet, like water, like a dream. A blue that is deep, mysterious, full of longing, this colour can take us through the depths of the oceans and beyond the sky and the mist of stars to infinity.

You will find in these pages the most important blues, ones that the all-time greatest painters have used in order to paint cloaks, mountains, Madonnas, angels, skies and storms. Guided by the words and illustrations in this book, you will discover the many meanings of blue and just some of the innumerable stories that bring it to life.

Throughout the book, you will find spaces to extend drawings, try out the suggested exercises, make your own sketches or notes and writing your impressions about what you see, notice and think. Make sure you always have a notebook with you so you never lose a creative idea or impression.

EGYPTIAN BLUE

The first blue was created by the ancient Egyptians, who obtained it by cooking a mixture of minerals at high temperature. It was the so-called Egyptian 'frit': the blue of ancient painting.

One example of such works is the group of blue monkeys frescoed on the walls of a building on the Greek island of Santorini, depicted climbing in a landscape of volcanic rocks similar to those in the ancient Thera.

Blue Monkeys (1700 BCE), National Archaeological Museum, Athens

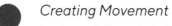

Creating Movement

Look carefully at their fluid, elegant movements and try to complete and extend the drawings using a blue pencil.

ULTRAMARINE

The king of blues is ultramarine which, in ancient times, was actually mined 'beyond the sea', as the name indicates, in the faraway quarries of Badakhshan, in Asia, by the source of the river Oxus – which the explorer Marco Polo described with great wonder as 'the best and finest in the world'.

Ultramarine comes from lapis lazuli, a blue mineral which, when ground and carefully refined, becomes a deep blue powder from which you obtain a colour so expensive that painters in the Middle Ages and the Renaissance used it sparingly. It was a colour as valuable as gold, therefore appropriate for the clothes of divine figures: first and foremost Mary, the mother of Jesus, and also the angels around her, like those around the Madonna painted for England's King Richard II.

The Wilton Diptych (1396–1399), National Gallery, London

Gold Amidst the Blue

Look at the colours in the painting and use any medium to colour in this outline in various shades of blue.

Inspired by the Lapis Lazuli Movement

Try to find a piece of lapls lazuli in a shop or online source selling semi-precious stones; they are quite easy to locate. If that's not possible, find an image on the internet and look at it onscreen. Examine it very carefully; take your time. You will see that the natural colour is not static but there are flecks of gold and tiny white spots in the deep blue.

See, or take inspiration from the colours and draw something from your imagination. Write notes on how you would describe the colour, what you would paint with it and how it makes you feel.

MADONNAS

Mary, the mother of Jesus, is frequently shown painted in precious lapis lazuli. Look online, in books or galleries and find some images that you find especially appealing of the Madonna wearing this intense blue. Copy them and make notes on the painterly qualities that using ultramarine brings to the subject. Then think about what you associate with the colour, such as calm, serenity and divinity.

Images of Motherhood

Can you find any other images of motherhood that use blue in similar – or very different – ways. Copy them and make notes to that show how the blue is used in the painting.

THE BEAUTY OF A BLUE SKY

Such spectacular effects could be obtained with lapis lazuli blue that one day, the artist Orazio Gentileschi, had a brilliant idea: why not paint directly onto a slab of lapis lazuli, leaving it exposed where needed? The result was a wonderful painting: a young David contemplating the head of Goliath, whom he has just killed, with ample space devoted to the sky and the lake behind him to show off the splendour and the various tones of the lapis lazuli.

Looking Up to Infinity

On a clear day, spend some time looking at the sky, then use watercolours to reproduce its various shades of blue.

Orazio Gentileschi, *David Contemplating the Head of Goliath* (1611–1616), Galleria Spada, Rome

BODY DECORATION

For a long time, clothes were dyed with woad, a lovely blue made from a plant, the *Isatis tinctoria*. The leaves were picked, ground, left to soak, then clumped into balls called *coques*, in French. The lands where these were produced became so wealthy that even now 'cockaigne' refers to a world of comfort and abundance.

The ancient Romans already knew about woad: Julius Caesar writes that Britons used woad to paint their bodies and faces blue to scare the enemy on the battlefield. In cultures all over the world and in every historical age, humans have decorated their bodies with ornamental patterns and colours, not only to go to war but also to pray, celebrate and for leisure.

Final Attack on Jerusalem (Tapestry, circa 1480),
Museo Nazionale del Bargello, Florence

Patterns and Colours on Clothing

What colours and patterns would you use on protective clothing to make you look more aggressive? Would you use blue or another colour? Would the shapes and patterns also have an influence on the effect? Sketch some ideas below.

Decorating Your Body

Using these human outlines, plan the kind of decoration you would like on your body, then colour them in. Create patterns for different occasions – perhaps one set of patterns to intimidate and enemy and one set designed to be attractive and welcoming. Which ideas are likely to succeed and which to fail?

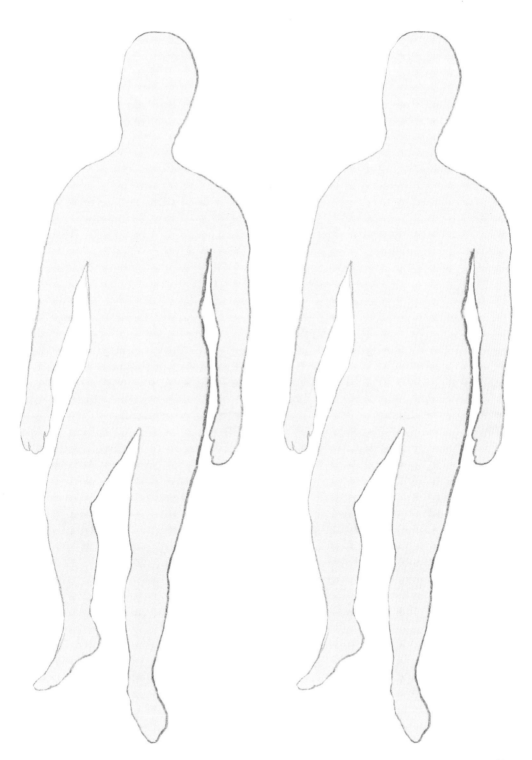

INDIGO

Woad was used until an even more beautiful and less expensive blue arrived in Europe: indigo. This colour was also obtained from a plant, the *Indigofera tinctoria*, which, as the name implies, originated in India. In order to avoid spoiling the woad trade, its use was forbidden for many years, but when indigo also started coming to Europe in large quantities also from the New World (the newly discovered America), it took over for good. How could you resist it, anyway? All you had to do was soak your fabric in a tub of indigo, then put it out to dry in order to obtain a beautiful, brightly coloured fabric, which was green for the first few minutes, then turned a deep blue.

John Constable, *Landscape with a Double Rainbow* (1812), Victoria and Albert Museum, London

Rainbows

Indigo is one of the seven colours of the rainbow: red, orange, yellow, green, blue, indigo, violet. Paint a rainbow, using as many different media as you can: watercolour, pastels, coloured pencils or another options you have available. Which do you think is best at conveying a realistic image? Which is more impactful?

WOVEN INDIGO

Indigo is the protagonist in another very famous story: in the middle of the 19th century, an enterprising young man called Levi Strauss decided to try selling a new stye of trousers made in a hard-wearing fabric dyed with indigo, which had been used for centuries in Europe to make ships' sails and sailors' clothes, and was perfect for anyone doing heavy work. It was known internationally by the name of the city in which it was produced, Genoa, or *Jeane* in old French. That is how the world's most famous trousers, blue jeans, came about.

Sewing in Blue
Copy the image opposite and colour it in with shades of blue.

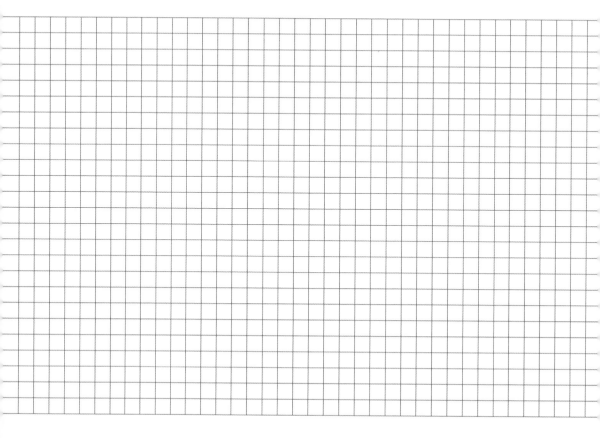

Master of the Tela Genova, *Mother Sewing and Two Children* (late 17th century), Fondazione Cariplo, Milan

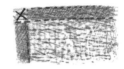

Blue Jeans

Most people have at least one pair of jeans in their wardrobe: pale, dark, skinny, wide, long, short. Look at the fabric carefully. You will see that that it is not uniformly indigo. The indigo threads form the warp of the garment – the threads that run the length of the fabric; the weft threads that run across the fabric are white. This makes the indigo dominate on one side and the white on the other. It also accounts for the varied colours of thread around a tear or on an edge. You will get further variations depending on the age of the jeans and how well-worn and well-washed they are.

Try to reproduce the various shades of the fabric, from the new pair, very dark, to the one that is more faded because of many washes, and the one that is really well worn.

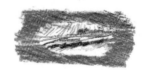

AZURITE

Another blue, azurite, originated in the German mountains and was often used instead of expensive ultramarine because it looked very similar but was one tenth of the cost. To avoid being cheated, buyers had to be very careful and would often check with their own eyes to make sure artists were not swindling them by using azurite instead of ultramarine.

Precisely because it was less expensive, azurite was the most widely used blue in antiquity and the Middle Ages: for example, we can admire a thousand shades of azurite in the wonderful painting below by the German artist Albrecht Dürer, in which the Madonna and her angels are distributing crowns of roses.

Albrecht Dürer, *Feast of the Rosary* (1506), National Gallery, Prague

Painting with Azurite

Use this blue to complete the painting, then devise your own group and paint the central figure in blue. You might want to look for inspiration to some other works by Albrecht Dürer.

PRUSSIAN BLUE

In the 18th century, a Berlin chemist discovered by chance how to produce a beautiful blue; he did not reveal his formula to anybody and became very rich by selling it. It was only many years later that an Englishman managed to discover his secret. Called 'Berlin blue' or 'Prussian blue' (Prussia is the state where the city of Berlin is located), it became an immediate favourite among artists because it made endless transparency and shades possible. For example, it was thanks to this blue that Canaletto succeeded in conveying on canvas the transparency of water, and not only in Venice, as this painting of an English landscape demonstrates.

Giovanni Antonio Canal, also known as Canaletto, *Old Walton Bridge* (1754), Dulwich Picture Gallery, London

Tones of Blue

See how many variations and tones of blue you can identify in Canaletto's painting, then make a palette to reproduce them by mixing the blue colour with a little white or a little black.

Use the various tones to reproduce the painting.

CORNFLOWER BLUE

With the advent of Prussian blue, blue triumphed not only in art but also in society. At the end of the 19th century, the antique dealer Stefano Bardini decided to paint the walls of his gallery a charming cornflower blue, the perfect backdrop to the works in his collection. His choice echoed throughout Europe and even beyond the Atlantic, so much so that a few years later, Isabel Stewart Gardner, an American collector, decided to use the same colour for the walls of her house in Boston and asked Bardini for the recipe to his inimitable blue.

Blue Room
Use the space below to sketch a room with blue walls.

Tino di Camaino, *Carità* (1320), Firenze, Museo Stefano Bardini

Using Background Colours

Have you ever thought about how a background colour can influence the way you see a work of art? Colour in the backgrounds to the sculpture in these outlines with green, yellow, violet or red. Compare them with the blue version. Pay attention to the various feelings you experience as you look at the different images and make notes on their visual impact and how they make you feel.

PICASSO IN BLUE

During the same years that Isabel Stewart was redesigning her house, the famous Spanish artist Pablo Picasso was having his 'blue period' (1901–1904). A midnight blue reigns over his paintings of that time and the protagonists express all their melancholy and anxiety: they are the poor, the sick, the old, beggars and prisoners who seem frozen in their sadness.

Tones of Blue

Look carefully at the work Picasso produced during the blue period and observe how he used blue tones on the paintings. You could make some sketches of the ones you find most effective and notes on the effects of blue.

Pablo Picasso (1901), *Woman in Blue*, Private Collection

Woman in Colours

The outlines opposite give you the opportunity to change the colours in the pictures. Try changing the colour of the dress or the background. Experiment with strong and subtle colours. It will soon be obvious the crucial role colour plays in any piece of artwork. You will realise how much colours can change the final result.

Next, draw a self-portrait below using a blue background.

BLUE TO CREATE INFINITY

During those same years, at the turn of the 20th century, the Russian artist Wassily Kandinsky painted a picture called *The Blue Rider*, in which a white horse with a rider in a blue cloak is galloping on a hill.

This painting gave its name to a group of artists – including Kandinsky – united in the belief that colours and shapes are full of spiritual values and that you could paint reality not just as it appears. They said about blue that. 'The deeper the blue, the more it evokes a sense of infinity, arousing a longing for purity and the supernatural ... If it is very dark, it gives a sense of calm. If it borders on black, it acquires a note of overwhelming sadness. If it veers towards lighter shades ..., on the other hand, it becomes indifferent and distant, like a very remote sky.'

Riding On
Continue Kandinsky's landscape on this page, imagining the places his blue rider will ride through.

Wassily Kandinsky, *The Blue Rider* (1903), Private Collection, Zurich

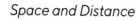

Space and Distance

Create a landscape in a similar style to the one on the previous spread but show a landscape of hills spreading into the distance. The further away the hills, the more blue they should appear in the picture. Use this to gain a long perspective.

THE COLOUR OF METAMORPHOSIS

According to the artist Jan Fabre, blue is the colour of metamorphosis, in which everything has happened, is about to happen and will happen. The blue hour is the hour of twilight, the time between day and night, when daytime animals are readying themselves to sleep while nocturnal animals are about to wake up. This is the time known as dusk, when the sun is sinking below the horizon and there are special light effects in the air.

This observation gave rise to a series of works produced with an ordinary ball-point pen, in which the artist managed to transform not only a canvas or a sheet of paper but also entire objects and expanses, even going as far as covering an entire castle with blue ink.

Jan Fabre, *Castle Tivoli* – Mechelen (1990)

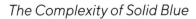

The Complexity of Solid Blue

Take a blue ball-point pen and fill this entire page, in blocks, using thick strokes close together in one place, lighter and sparser strokes elsewhere; introduce as much variety as you can. When you have filled the page, you will realise that it only takes a ball-point pen to create a world.

NIGHT SKIES

As night falls, blue reigns supreme once again: a deep blue, almost black, in which we could get lost if there were no stars to guide us. The starry sky has inspired poets and artists of every era and even now we are all of us bewitched by the spectacle of the night; surrounded by this deep, silent blue, we cannot help but wonder what is up there, beyond the atmosphere, beyond the solar system, beyond the universe.

Giotto, *Scrovegni Chapel* (1303–1304), Padua

Ever Changing, Always the Same

It will not be hard for you to find famous night skies in books or on the internet. Giotto's or Van Gogh's, for example. Look at them carefully, starting with the Giotto. What impresses you about the colour? How many tones of blue can you see? Is the use of colour subtle or bold? Choose what inspiration you would take from this painting, make notes on your impressions and draw your version of the sky.

Modern Skies

Now look at one of Van Gogh's famous starry skies. Think about the emotion behind the colours – what do they represent to you? Do your own version of one of Van Gogh's paintings that are predominantly blue.

Vincent Van Gogh, *Starry Night Over the Rhône* (1888), Musée d'Orsay, Paris

Creating a Backdrop

Now compare the previous skies to the one Karl Friedrich Schinkel painted for the set of Mozart's *Magic Flute*. What differences can you see? What are the similarities? Create your own stage backdrop of a starry sky.

Karl Friedrich Schinkel, *The Queen of the Night* (1815)

QUESTIONING THE MEANING

René Magritte, a Belgian artist for whom the entire world was a source of amazement, often painted the sky just at the moment when the night gives way to light, a pale light that bewitches us and leaves us suspended. His works, both very sharp and mysterious, arouse questions about the meaning of art and objects.

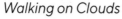

Walking on Clouds
Magritte did not want to paint reality; what he was interested in was painting the need for mystery. Look at this painting carefully: what do you think the two characters suspended among the clouds are saying to each other? Try to imagine their dialogue and, to encourage your creativity, colour in the clouds.

René Magritte, *The Infinite Recognition* (1963), Private Collection

PAINTING WITH YOUR WHOLE BODY

Even though he had a large number of blue pigments to choose from, the painter Yves Klein was never satisfied; no matter what binder he mixed it with, he thought the blue lost its purity and intensity. He therefore got to work and found a synthetic resin that preserved all the pigment's luminosity. A new blue was born: the International Klein Blue, which the artist patented, proudly proclaiming the advent of a Blue Epoch.

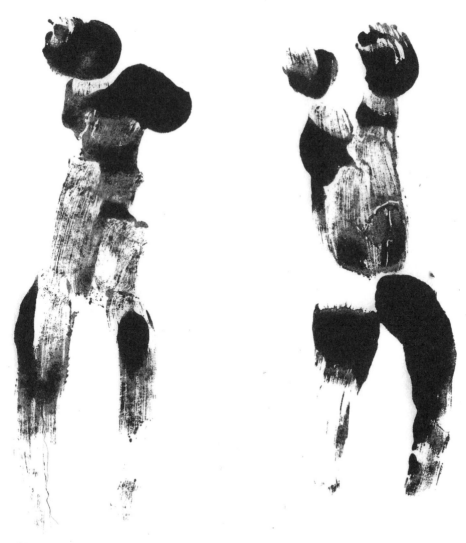

The colour was spread on canvas with rollers and sponges but that was not all. Klein asked models to become 'tools' and leave the mark of their bodies on the canvas.

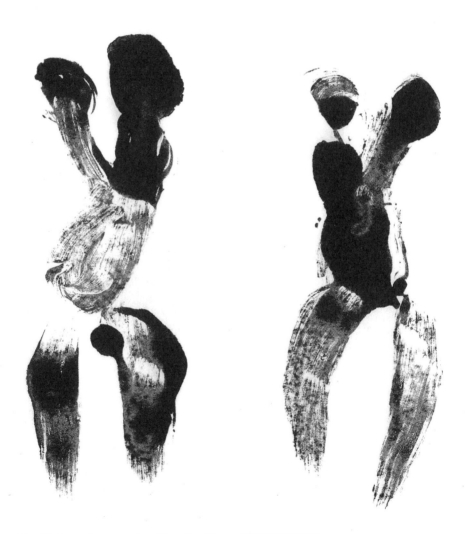

Yves Klein, *Anthropometry of the Blue Period* (ANT 82) (1960), Musée National d'Art Moderne, Centre George Pompidou, Paris

Body Prints

You, too, can spread some blue watercolour on a part of your body and leave its mark on a sheet of paper. Try different tones of blue and textures of paint and see what kind of results you can achieve.

PAINTING IN BLUE

As a final project in your study of blue, try to think about how many blue things you know and make some lists on the following pages under the headings provided or by making up your own.

From the electric blue of cornflowers to the deep turquoise of a tropical ocean. From the Smurfs to delicate china cups. From a police officer's uniform to a nurse's scrubs blue can mean 'purity', 'safety' or 'cleanliness', so dear to science; in Anglo-Saxon countries, blue is a word for melancholy. All these different connotations should encourage you to see just how important a colour blue is. it is around us all the time both in plain sight – the overarching sky above – and concealed in more valuable objects – like a precious item of china of the feathers on a peacock.

People

Think about the significance of blue when applied to people. It may indicate calm or purity. For many centuries, blue was the colour of aristocracy, and it is also often associated with scientists and health; notice how many medicines have a packaging of this colour. Navy blue is a favourite colour for clothes, especially uniforms. In ancient Japan, it was worn by firefighters and fishermen and nowadays it is worn worldwide by sailors and for elegant formal suits. Draw some of your own blue people below.

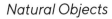

Natural Objects

The sky and the ocean are the most obvious items to top this list, but there are many more. From sapphires and lapis lazuli to the bright plumage of jungle birds, from ripe blueberries and beautiful cornflowers, look around you to find the blue in your natural surroundings. Draw some natural blue objects below.

Man-made Objects

From the transparent blue of swimming pools to blue glass, fabrics or painted china, you will find blue used everywhere. Think about how you use it in our home and possessions and the atmosphere it creates. Draw some blue items from your home below.

WHERE TO FIND OUT MORE

There is an infinite resource of images and information on the internet just waiting to be discovered. Here are just a few places you might start to find out more about some of the pieces of artwork in this book.

Art Gallery of NSW, Sydney, artgallery.nsw.gov.au

Cariplo Foundation, Milan, fondazionecriplo.it

Galleria Spada, Rome, galleriaspada.beniculturali.it

Isabel Stewart Gardner Museum, gardnermuseum.org

Musée National d'Art Moderne, Centre George Pompidou, Paris, centrepompidou.fr/en

Musée d'Orsay, Paris, m.musee-orsay.fr/en

Museo Nazionale del Bargello, Florence, bargellomusel.beneculturali.it

Museo Stefano Bardini, Firenze, museicivicifiorentini,cnnnbe,fi.it

National Gallery, London, nationalgallery.org.uk

National Gallery, Prague, ngprague.cz

National Gallery of Australia, nga.gov.au

Palazzo Vecchio, florenceartmuseums.com/palazzo-vecchio

Scrovegni Chapel, cappelladegliscrovegni.it/index.php/en/

Victoria and Albert Museum, London,vam.ac.uk

Giotto, giottodibondone.org

Jan Fabre, janfabre.de

Wassily Kandinsky, www.wassilykandinsky.net

Yves Klein, yvesklein.com/en

René Magritte, renemagritte.org

Henri Matisse, henrimatissse.org

Pablo Picasso, museupocasso.bcn.cat, museopicassomalaga.org

Karl Friedrich Schinkel, karl-friedrich-schinkel.com

Vincent Van Gogh, vangoghmuseum.nl

ACKNOWLEDGEMENTS:
The Italian publishers would like to thank MUS.E and Giotto FILA, who
partnered with them to make these books possible.

This English language edition Published in 2021 by OH!,
an imprint of Welbeck Non-Fiction Limited,
part of Welbeck Publishing Group
20 Mortimer Street
London W1T 3JW
English Translation by © Welbeck Non-Fiction Limited

First published by © Topipittori Milan in 2017
Original title: *Blu*
www.topipittori.it

Blu by Valentina Zucchi and Viola Niccolai
ISBN 978-1-80069-013-4

Text © Valentina Zucchi and Viola Niccolai
Translator: Katherine Gregor
Editorial: Wendy Hobson
Design: Nikki Ellis
Production: Rachel Burgess

A CIP catalogue record for this book is available from the British Library

Printed and bound in China by Leo Paper Products Ltd.

10 9 8 7 6 5 4 3 2 1